The Essential Handbook and Professional Chang

MW01165506

The Prodigal Principle

WORTHBOOKS™
PUBLISHING GROUP, INC.

18 Biltmore Park
Bloomfield, CT 06002-2141

THE PRODIGAL PRINCIPLE: The Essential Handbook for Managing Personal and Professional Change. Copyright © 1995 by Martis Jones, Ph.D. Copyright under International, Pan American and Universal Copyright Conventions. All rights reserved. No part of this book may be reproduced or transmitted in any form or by any means, electronic or mechanical, including photocopying, recording, or by any information storage and retrieval system, without permission in writing from the Publisher.

WORTHBOOKS™
PUBLISHING GROUP, INC.

18 Biltmore Park, Bloomfield, CT 06002-2141

Substantial discounts on bulk quantities of The Prodigal Principle are available to corporations, professional associations and other organizations. For details and discount information, contact the sales office at Worthbooks™ Publishing Group, Inc., 214-243-2524; Fax 214-243-2504.

All names and other superficial details have been altered to preserve the confidentiality of both individuals and the organizations whose cases are discussed in this book.

Manufactured in the United States of America.
This book is printed on acid-free paper.

Library of Congress Cataloging-in-Publication Data

Jones, Martis

The Prodigal Principle: the essential handbook for managing personal and professional change/Martis Jones

p. cm. - (The Worthbooks™ personal management series)

Includes index
ISBN 0-9644607-1-8
1. Personal change management - How to
2. Professional change management - the individual
3. Personal development
4. Organizational change - Human development aspects
5. Unemployment - Psychological aspects
6. Healthy lifestyle - How to
I. Title   II. Series

Library of Congress Catalog Card Number: 94-61929
Printed in the United States of America
First Edition
WPG 10 9 8 7 6 5 4 3 2 1

CONTENTS

DEDICATION

Many thanks to the triumphant champions of change who shared their personal stories so that others might grow and change their lives from them.

To all the readers of my professional materials and publications; and to companies and professional organizations that have invited me to speak about managing personal change. Also to all the major corporations where I worked as an executive. Thank you for the numerous professional projects I was privileged to conduct and manage for you in organizational change, executive education, management development and personal change management.

Dr. Martis Jones

PREFACE

Look no more outside yourself for infinite powers and treasures. Open your eyes and turn inward to the unlimited treasure house within you — your own mind. There you will find an infinite supply of joy, happiness, peace, wisdom, health, wealth, creativity and power. You don't need to acquire it. It's there already. Believe in it. Look inside and find it. Use it.

This book uses the metaphor of **home** as a condition of your thinking. In its ideal, your mind serves you as a treasure house of good. **Home**, as used in this book, is not a physical dwelling place. It is not a raised ranch, an apartment, a condominium, a duplex or an estate. **Home** is a state of mind. The ideal **home** is the mind in a state of well-being. It is a safe place where you can look for answers to all you desire. It is a state of mind in which you accept yourself as a worthwhile, beautiful, creative, peaceful, prosperous and connected person with an endless supply of good, for you to enjoy and share with others. When you are at **home**, your mind is your safe haven. It dwells within you. Staying at **home** keeps you aware of your internal qualities — joy, love, power, intelligence, creativity, happiness, balance and health — versus merely acquiring material things in the outer world.

Tool Box

In this book, you will find *home tools* (⬤) that show you quick methods and techniques for making essential changes and building a new lifestyle. You will find them enlightening and easy to use. Your *power practices* (✐) are exercises to raise questions, arouse deeper searching and help you continue to build and cement new lifestyle habits and patterns. These thought-provoking exercises will help you find **home** and stay there to continually grow and stay bigger than the circumstances outside you. You will learn how to excel as a champion in these turbulent times we face today and in the 21st century.

Use this book to find contentment and balance in your personal life, at work and in other areas. Most of all, use it to master one of the highest levels of human achievement — taking care of yourself, while making an impact in your community. Search no more the world over to find **home**. Find answers in *The Prodigal Principle* to help you turn within and find **home**.

WELCOME

T his handbook is your personal *how to* guide for thriving in these unpredictable, tough times. Learn to use this handbook to achieve balance and excel as you face the constant changes in your life. You will find this special guide helpful when you are challenged by any extreme circumstances — dysfunctional job, family conflict, bad relationships, burnout, stress, lack of intimacy, fledgling or floundering business, or eating, smoking or drinking too much.

You will also find your special place in this handbook when you want confirmation that you are doing okay and maintaining balance and inner peace. Clever quotes and wise sayings from scholars and sages of our times will teach you and energize you. This handbook will reinforce your positive steps and encourage you to continue taking them.

As you read these pages, you will be inspired, informed and assured by the simple yet powerful tools and guidelines. The true stories in this handbook are told by everyday people such as you and me; people who have encountered problems and crises and taken them as cues to rebuild their attitudes and approaches to life and work. They reinvented their thinking and triumphed in turbulent times. They overcame and achieved extraordinary results. You will find their stories compelling and memorable. You will find yourself in these stories; and they will inspire you to begin your own journey back home to better balance. Embrace them and read them over and over again.

This handbook covers all of the topics you have been looking for to help you find meaning and decide what to do next in your life — your career; your relationships with your family, loved ones and co-workers; your health; and your personal life. This handbook gives true meaning to the phrase *there for you*, and covers such topics as:

➡ Recovering from failure
➡ Securing your employability
➡ Reinventing your lifestyles patterns in personal, home and work areas of life
➡ Building support systems and alliances
➡ Preventing stagnation
➡ Building stamina and endurance
➡ Designing a lifelong success plan
➡ Transforming your life
➡ Reclaiming creativity

This is a straightforward and pragmatic handbook. Use it. It's yours. Write in the margins. Scribble and draw. Use it as a journal. Make it your constant companion, your sourcebook, your pocket book, your pocket pal, your desk reference, your bedside reading mate. It will give you steady support, encouragement and guidance as you face life's uncertainties.

Chapter

1

What Now?
Surviving the Nineties

> *The world breaks everyone*
> *and afterward many are strong*
> *at the broken places.*
> — ERNEST HEMINGWAY

Restructuring. Downsizing. Rightsizing. Reorganizing. Call it what you want. The traditional model of the workplace is gone. It has vanished. Kaput. There is no more 45-year job. No more 25-year Rolex watch, grandfather's clock or 14-karat gold ring. No more luxury company car. No more golf or country club membership. No more guaranteed retirement or pension plans. There are fewer sole-breadwinner fathers and stay-at-home bread-baker mothers. Beaver Cleaver families and Dagwood Bumstead jobs have vanished.

As we are hurled toward the year 2000, a *jobquake* is dismantling the workplace and breaking up the old rules of jobs, promotions and careers (*Fortune*). The last wave — the job tidal wave — has washed us ashore to the entrance of a new era of unfamiliar work

3 THE PRODIGAL PRINCIPLE

assignments with new risks. We face the dawning of a new golden era of people-sizing, and retrofitting the displaced worker for a changed world of new roles and new rules for contemporary careers and lifelong learning.

Ready or not, the post-job worker will need to prepare to break into this strange world of employment. Referred to as a *de-jobbed* workplace (*Fortune*), this new era rings in exciting opportunities for lifelong learning. Preparing oneself with lifetime skills and knowledge portfolio development versus the static resumé will be the norm. Ready or not, these evolutionary workplace challenges will clearly separate gazelles from dinosaurs. The lynx-eyed survivors will quickly separate themselves from the extinct.

2

What Next?
Thriving in the 21st Century

> *The future enters into us*
> *in order to transform itself in us,*
> *long before it happens.*
> — RAINER MARIA RILKE

This chapter gives year 2000 trends for the workplace, work groups and for the individual. Here are some of the most prominent year 2000 trends in the workplace.

TRENDS FOR THE ORGANIZATION

➤ Major organizations will reorganize more than two times in any given year.

➤ Corporate hierarchy will get shorter and slimmer.

➤ The 45-year job will go away.

➤ A *de-jobbed* workplace means that more and more work will be handled by contract labor, part-timers and temporary labor. Flex-time, telecommuting and job sharing will be common.

➤ Middle management will continue to disappear. Teams and self-directed work groups will fill the void.

➤ Fifty to 60-hour work weeks will be common.

➤ More than 50 percent of 1990s full-time workers will drop off corporate payrolls.

TRENDS FOR THE WORK GROUP

➤ The new worker will be hired for the project, for fixed periods of time and then on to the next project.

➤ *It's not my job* attitudes will no longer be acceptable. The *de-jobbed* worker will wear many hats and present herself or himself as multi-skilled.

➤ Traditional bosses will be outmoded. Workers will be self-directed and guided by the demands of the project, work team, customers and vendors.

➤ Extensive supervisory training programs will disappear. Team leaders will be prepared to communicate as coaches, supporters, buffers and brokers. They will nurture and facilitate. They will promote harmony and creativity among members of the work team.

TRENDS FOR THE INDIVIDUAL

➤ There will be no more promises of permanent 40-hour job stability.

➤ Everything will be new for the year-2000 worker. New teams. New team members. New team leaders. New faces. New assignments. New skills. New customers. New suppliers. New contract laborers. New workplaces. New ways of working and completing assignments. New kinds of employment opportunities.

➤ Workplace watchwords will be *increase* and *decrease*, and workers will be expected to do both simultaneously. Payrolls will shrink at the same time. Workloads will increase beyond our imaginings. The new worker will be expected to increase profit margins and merchandise sales and expand products and services. The *de-jobbed* worker will be given faster production schedules, more travel and more work hours. He or she will be expected to decrease spending on all fronts, reduce labor costs, decrease expense accounts, reduce staffing, reduce the cost of doing business.

➤ Loyalty to the company will be replaced by loyalty to self, to personal values, to the family and work team members.

➤ Elements of personal lifestyles will show signs of *increase* and *decrease*. Individuals and families will learn how to *cash out* (*The*

Popcorn Report) and work for new meaning. This might mean working for less to gain greater self-satisfaction, peace of mind and sense of high self-worth.

➤ Instead of signing long-term employment contracts, the new workers will sign temporary, part-time or contract labor agreements. Many will work out of their homes as corporate employees and noncorporate entrepreneurs.

➤ The new worker will plan his or her lifetime portfolio for at least 20 years beyond the typical retirement age (55-65).

➤ Doing more with less will require employees to maximize their creative and organizational skills.

➤ Constant turnover will produce fewer mentors. Veterans will have less time for mentoring.

➤ Workers with outmoded approaches, outdated skills and narrow experience will paint themselves out of the modern workplace.

➤ Individuals will need to take responsibility for personal development. They will attend programs in personal energy management, stress management, balancing home and work, burnout prevention and personal change management.

➤ Smart employees will not wait for the organization to train them and make them marketable. They will seize opportunities to learn new skills, and they will present them at the employment bargaining table.

➤ Workplace trends will impact other areas of our personal lives, including health, family relationships, emotional, spiritual, intellectual and cultural patterns. Individuals will participate in personal development programs to search for a better quality of life and to achieve balance.

➤ Family will become more important. People will prepare their homes as safe havens — places for comfort, peace, joy, warmth, protection, relaxation and general well-being.

➤ People will want to live longer and live well. They will seek health and well-being. They will work for better quality in work life and family life.

Call the world if you Please
'The vale of Soul-making.'
— JOHN KEATS

✐ Here is some *power practice*:

1. In what ways have these trends changed how you view work?

_____
_____
_____
_____

2. In what ways have these trends created changes in how you do your work?

_____
_____
_____
_____

3. Do you find joy in your work?

_____
_____
_____
_____

4. If you were to start a new kind of work today, what difference would it make (in your life and the lives of your loved ones — financial, quality of life, health, leisure time, emotional, spiritual, cultural activities)?

_____
_____
_____
_____

5. What does loyalty mean to you? Define loyalty.

_____
_____
_____
_____

The proper work for our species at this time
in history is work on ourselves.
— E. F. SCHUMACHER

3

New Responsibilities
and Opportunities

*We only want that which is given naturally to all peoples
of the world, to be masters of our own fate.*

— GOLDA F. MEIR

Corporate America cannot move forward with burned-out, stressed-out and worn-out workers. Restructuring, downsizing, rightsizing and reorganizing will not work if employees' minds and attitudes are not there or not healthy enough to meet the constant changes. A 1994 study by the United Healthcare Corporation of Minnetonka, Minn., found high employee stress levels contributing to low productivity. Seventy-two percent of the employees had noticed co-workers handling personal issues on company time. To make job changes work, corporations and organizations now need to train and develop energetic, well-balanced, focused, creative and healthy workers to meet the current and 21st century workplace changes. They will need to educate, train, re-train, rejuvenate, revitalize and renew American workers. Some companies are not ready to assign the necessary resources to support the personal needs of their employees, and you can't wait.

You must take charge and stay in charge of your employability. If you cannot wait for your company to help you, you can start with this handbook and help yourself. If you are an entrepreneur or are among the "self-bossed," you will also find the following ideas useful for championing personal change.

The purpose of this handbook is to show you:

➟ how to re-make your attitude and see the positive side of change
➟ how to gain whole-person balance
➟ how to build healthy lifestyle patterns
➟ how to convert your work to your *worth*
➟ how to secure your employability

You will no longer be satisfied to join the couch potatoes once you have followed the ideas in this handbook. No more will you marinate your mind with avoidance-seeking pastimes. No more will you continue to allow yourself to succumb to self-defeating thinking, dullness or unconscious negative habits. You will stop depending on someone else to do for you what you are capable of doing for yourself — taking control and getting your life back in balance.

As you begin, you will take baby steps. Later, you will take giant leaps to manage challenges and crises in your job, your business, your financial matters, relationships with your family and co-workers, or relating to your health or spirituality. You will emerge brand new, creative, clearly focused and directed with purpose, courage and determination. You will be prepared to succeed in the new *dejobbed* workplace and beyond.

You will turn Monday morning blues into everyday hurrahs. You will set yourself ahead of those choosing to lag behind and become extinct. You will craft your own life plan by converting your work to your *worth*. Keeping a healthy balance in work and family will become an everyday way of life for you. Living a healthy lifestyle will become your daily practice.

Let's get started.

Chapter

4

Separating the Survivors
from the Extinct

> *It's not whether you get knocked down.*
> *It's whether you get up again.*
> — VINCE LOMBARDI

As frightening, challenging or encouraging as work, family and individual trends may seem to you, they sound a drum roll and hurdle us into the 21st century. How will you get there? What's in it for you? The true stories in this chapter will help you answer these questions.

Today's and tomorrow's workers will need to keep emotionally, attitudinally and physically fit to keep up with the swift changes they face in fast-moving organizations. They can't continue to practice common negative coping behaviors such as denial or withdrawal:

Denial is a form of grieving that healthy people use to protect themselves from pain. It becomes harmful when we practice it for too long. For example, when Fred was laid off, he continued to show up for work each day. He had to go through counseling to learn to accept his loss and find a new career direction.

Withdrawal is another natural behavior we practice to protect ourselves when we experience a loss. When Shirley's department was expanded to 50 people, she was devastated. She had never managed more than three people. Although curious and creative before, with this added pressure she lost interest and began to run her job on auto pilot. Her common answer to every question became "great." She became detached. At home, she found herself going to bed earlier and earlier. Shirley soon resigned from her management job and found a customer service position with a small retailer. Although earning less money, she has time to think about what matters to her and what she is really good at. She is also reclaiming her joy.

Practiced for too long, denial and withdrawal create stress, burnout, *dis-ease* and sickness, including stroke, headaches, stomachaches and heart attack. Research shows that the majority of heart attacks in America strike between Sunday afternoon and Monday afternoon. Monday is found to be not only blue, but also the worst day of the workweek for stress. Between Sunday afternoon and Sunday night, over 60 percent of American workers squash the thought of getting out of bed and going to work on Monday morning. They seek to numb their misery through television, alcohol, drugs, violence, sex or complete withdrawal.

The thrivers find ways to champion changes. Consider Colvin, 36. He knew he was about to be laid off from his hotel management job. He began a new business venture and opened a restaurant. He earns far less than he did working for the hotel, but loves what he is doing and knows in time he will turn a profit.

A family of five, with one disabled child and another recovering from injuries from an automobile accident, cashed out and moved to the hills of Vermont to start an antiques business, enjoy the slower pace and each other. They said less is more. Even though they have reduced their income, they enjoy the benefits of quality time as a loving and nurturing family unit.

Scott created a whirlwind of success in his investment banking career. Longing to do something he could enjoy, he cashed out and found a teaching job at an Ivy League business school. He combined teaching with a doctoral program and rose to become a full professor of international banking.

Clark ran a successful business until it went belly up. Depressed and despondent, he struggled with severe depression for over half a year. Then he got his wind again. He knew his business, but lacked management skills. He found his way back through business training, a lot of time thinking and reflecting on his successes, support from family and friends and rebuilding his courage to go back out and win. Today, his business is back on track and showing record profits.

Audrey and her family are doing a lot of juggling to help her change her career from teacher to lawyer. As her husband arrives home from work, she turns over their two toddlers to him as she scoots off for school. When she arrives home from law school, he leaves for his moonlighting job with a janitorial service. It is a difficult schedule, but both recognize and have invested in the long-term rewards.

Pam was divorced and lost her job in a two-month period. She was left with two teenagers to rear. She felt trapped. She found solace with friends, family and other supporters who served as her catalysts, coaches and cheering squad. She sought job counseling and learned what skills she would need to change careers and set new job goals. Pam found her perfect job working for a local hospital.

Glenn, age 48, went to work, set up shop, and in the same hour was told to empty his desk. The news hit him like a tidal wave. Teetering in the wake, he asked himself, "Who will hire a dinosaur like me?" His answer was, "I will." He soon started an investment service business and learned how to make it profitable. He said, "The best thing that happened to me was being fired. I had always been successful but didn't know why or how. Being out on my own has taught me to look at myself, take inventory and continue to grow."

There are many more stories to tell about champions of change. In summary, everyone is facing a job change — recently laid off, soon to be laid off, starting a new business or learning to do business better.

Apply these *home tools:*

1. Face what is happening. Grieve if you must. Feel angry or stymied. Then pick yourself up, dust yourself off and go take your turn in the employment world.

2. Know yourself. Face your strengths and opportunities. Find ways to plug into your strengths and sharpen your skills. Know specifically what you want and how to get it.

3. Network like you never did before. Write down all of your contacts — friends, colleagues, neighbors, business associates, club members, board members, church members, spheres of influence. Don't be shy. Tell everyone what you want to do and help them help you get there. If anyone says he or she can't help you, ask for someone who can.

4. Craft the most creative resumé and cover letter possible. Circulate them. Some people create resumé business cards and pass them out at networking functions.

5. Market yourself and hire yourself as your best public relations manager. Cultivate prospects, interview at your best, follow up and remember to always say, "Thank you" and "Please."

Despite the uncertainty and nanosecond change we face, we have ways to thrive and transform our lives. We can magnify our possibilities by feeling our own hope, inner peace, joy, courage and commitment to ourselves.

✐ Here is some *power practice*:

Stop and find a quiet place to do some inner work. Ask yourself these questions. Write your answers.

1. What's going on in my life right now?

_____
_____
_____

2. How do I feel about my situation?

_____
_____
_____

3. What am I willing to do about my situation?

_____
_____
_____

4. Who will help me?

_____
_____
_____

Lessons in Survival

Every morning in Africa, a gazelle wakes up knowing it must run faster than the fastest lion or be killed. Every morning a lion awakens knowing it must outrun the slowest gazelle or starve to death. It doesn't matter if you are a lion or a gazelle. When the sun comes up, you'd better be running.

— ANONYMOUS

Chapter

5

The Corporate Son

> To keep a lamp burning, we have to put oil in it.
> — MOTHER TERESA

Greg's story will help you understand the importance of changing your lifestyle to succeed in the new American world of work. Before his recent transformation, Greg, vice president of operations for a national retailer, carved a path from home to work and back home to cocoon as a couch potato. Although the demands in his business changed, Greg stayed the same — pushing the same worn-out programs and ideas. He addressed problems and programs mechanically, showing no creativity. He felt dull and out of touch with the business. Five years of this destructive lifestyle pattern turned Greg into a cynical, burned-out person.

To numb his feelings of unhappiness and despair, Greg turned to television. He lay securely on the sofa night after night, hypnotizing himself with televised talk shows, infomercials and sports. He sought comfort in salty snacks, heavy desserts and beer. Cocooning in his couch-potato lifestyle, Greg was not aware of how much change had engulfed him or how destructive his coping methods had become.

His company reorganized. When he learned that he was responsible for a larger geographic area and fewer employees, Greg felt stunned. He ended up on a different path — starting with the emergency room, the operating room and the intensive care unit of his local hospital. One of his arteries was 95 percent blocked. After recovering from an angioplasty, Greg decided to change his lifestyle.

He knew that his surgery was merely a bandage covering a bigger underlying problem. He knew that unless he fixed it, the problem would return and eventually lead to his death. He began to examine his whole life, starting with his attitude, his work, eating habits and other lifestyle patterns.

He soon learned that the old way he ran his life when it was job-based no longer worked. Several times he asked himself if he liked his work well enough to continue doing it. He answered, "Yes," but he also knew he would have to work differently. The job he had been trained to do 20 years ago was one he no longer recognized. Greg began to plan his new work portfolio. His plans did not include working as vice president. He also addressed issues in his personal life. He went through a healthy-lifestyle counseling program. He set new priorities.

He committed himself to changing his diet, losing 50 pounds, getting off the couch, beginning an exercise program, giving up cigarettes, finding a healthy-lifestyle support group and registering for a stress management course. He sought career counseling in an outplacement center and reassessed his strengths and qualifications. He decided to work as an entrepreneur.

Today, after three years of lifesaving changes, Greg runs a consulting company that advises his former company and other Fortune 500 companies on sales and marketing innovations. He walks or does NordicTrack daily, sets aside a lot of thinking time and does yoga every day. He follows a vegetarian diet, eats little fat and continues to meet with his healthy-heart support group. Greg said that he has emerged from the cocoon renewed, clear-eyed and stronger. "I show no evidence of blockage in my heart or my creativity. I start and end each day with energy to burn, clear purpose and an ardent desire to continue my total-person balanced lifestyle," he said. He adds that he works more enthusiastically and accomplishes more than ever before, more than he ever imagined. He thrives on zest and zeal for his work and his personal life. He said that he made major lifestyle changes and "got a life." Most important, he said he got an "inner life."

There are many transformed Gregs. They know that the paradigm of business continues to shift and work continues to be redefined. They have committed themselves to constantly learning and growing; doing more analyzing, evaluating and extrapolating; and constantly re-evaluating their lives and facing themselves.

What lies behind us and what lies before us are tiny matters compared to what lies within us.
— RALPH WALDO EMERSON

✐ Use this *power practice*:

1. In what ways are you rethinking, reinventing, rebuilding or changing the way you work?_____

_____

_____

_____

_____

_____

2. In what ways will your new way of working make a difference (for you and others)?_____

_____

_____

_____

_____

_____

3. In what ways are you rethinking, reinventing, rebuilding or changing your lifestyle (personal, family, health, finances)?_____

_____

_____

_____

_____

_____

4. Whom will you ask to help you?_____

_____

_____

_____

_____

_____

5. What are your related strengths?_____

_____

_____

_____

_____

_____

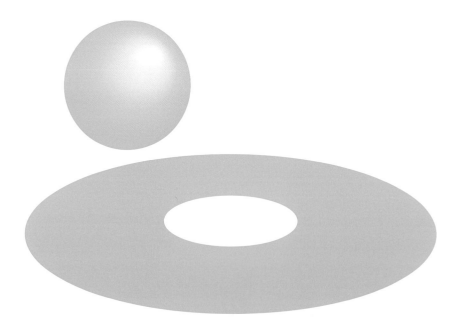

Chapter

6

The Prodigal Principle

> *Unless man (or woman) has a natural bent*
> *in accordance with nature's, he (or she)*
> *has no chance of understanding nature at all.*
> — WALTER PATER

N ow let's turn to a simple secret for making changes in your personal affairs and work life. It is *The Prodigal Principle*. The main teaching of *The Prodigal Principle* is:

**When we reach an extreme condition
in our life,
we are quickened to transform and heal.**

Extreme Condition + Quickening = Transformation

When we stay weighted down by our negative habit patterns, we become burdened. The weight of our awareness makes us heavy. Engulfed by our awareness, we sink into self-destructive circumstances. Over time, we end up in a negative extreme. This is when we experience states of suffering and *dis-ease*.

The key is to break the destructive habit patterns and begin constructive steps. When we do, we lighten our load and begin the return home to our treasure house. A changed awareness restores our vision of good, helps us see possibilities, renews our thinking and redirects our approach. We champion breakthroughs to transform and heal our negative condition. What emerges on the other side is a miraculous, brand-new person reaching forward as never before — showing clear vision of now and the future, clear values, a new direction, and new-found abilities to achieve more than ever imagined.

The human spirit has a power to turn insufficiency into awareness of abundance, strength, intuition and inspiration. Use *The Prodigal Principle* to heal yourself, to prevent unnecessary suffering, and complete transformations in your personal life and in your work. Just as countless others who have successfully used *The Prodigal Principle,* you will learn sure-fire ways out of the extremes in your life and you will achieve greater personal balance. Start now and put the brakes on your rapid rat race, quit burning yourself out, sharpen your positive awareness, and make the kinds of choices that keep you balanced and out of the extremes.

Understanding The Prodigal Principle

Applying *The Prodigal Principle* begins by understanding some basic terminology. The first is *when.* Destructive behavior can become so ingrained that you are not aware of what you are doing. *When* connotes that some time has elapsed to bring you to an extreme. *When* also points to an experience in "nowness" and means that once you recognize your negative habit patterns, you must develop a positive awareness and begin to make the necessary changes.

Another part of the principle is *an extreme condition.* An extreme condition could occur in any area of your life — involving children, health, your spouse, friends, work, money or spiritual matters. The condition could manifest itself as burnout, insomnia, sickness, impotence, backaches, bankruptcy, stomachaches or a general state of *dis-ease.*

> *We are healed of our suffering only by experiencing it to the full.*
> — MARCEL PROUST

✐ Use this *power practice*:

1. How do you reach the extremes in your life?

_____

_____

_____

_____

2. What are your quickenings (warning signals or triggers)?

_____

_____

_____

3. What do you do when you get quickenings?

_____

_____

_____

4. How do you respond to these warning signals?

_____

_____

_____

_____

5. How do you restore balance?

_____

_____

_____

6. How do you stay balanced?

_____

_____

_____

An extreme condition is created when you do not heed the warnings, and you allow negative conditions to push you off balance and out of control. What are some of your extremes? Take the **Personal Lifestyle Assessment**™ questionnaire (page 22) and discover in what areas you might want to begin to change your awareness.

PERSONAL LIFESTYLE ASSESSMENT™

Directions: As you can see, each scale below is composed of a pair of adjectives or phrases. Each pair represents two kinds of contrasting behavior. Circle the number that most closely represents what's going on in your life now. Add your scores to get your total.

1. Happy with my job	0 1 2 3 4 5 6 7 8 9 10	Hate my job
2. In excellent health	0 1 2 3 4 5 6 7 8 9 10	Experience bad health
3. Eat a healthful, balanced diet (vegetables, fruit, whole grains, beans, rice)	0 1 2 3 4 5 6 7 8 9 10	Eat too much less healthful food (fat, salt, sugar, white flour, fried food, salty snacks)
4. Do not smoke	0 1 2 3 4 5 6 7 8 9 10	Smoke too much
5. Get plenty of sound sleep	0 1 2 3 4 5 6 7 8 9 10	Insomnia (very little sleep)
6. Have happy relationships with my family	0 1 2 3 4 5 6 7 8 9 10	Family relationships defined by constant conflict
7. Work regular hours	0 1 2 3 4 5 6 7 8 9 10	Work lots of hours and/or bring work home (more than 60 hours per week)
8. Have high tolerance of ambiguity	0 1 2 3 4 5 6 7 8 9 10	Need to see things in black and white
9. Resolve conflicts	0 1 2 3 4 5 6 7 8 9 10	Avoid conflicts
10. See the good side of circumstances	0 1 2 3 4 5 6 7 8 9 10	See the negative side of circumstances
11. Feel little need to control others	0 1 2 3 4 5 6 7 8 9 10	Feel great need to control others
12. See life as rewarding	0 1 2 3 4 5 6 7 8 9 10	See life as punishing
13. Need short recovery time after adversity or disappointment	0 1 2 3 4 5 6 7 8 9 10	Take long recovery time after adversity or disappointment
14. Rely on nurturing relationships for support	0 1 2 3 4 5 6 7 8 9 10	Take matters into my own hands without help from others
15. Listen effectively	0 1 2 3 4 5 6 7 8 9 10	Interrupt others
16. Think about "what's important now"	0 1 2 3 4 5 6 7 8 9 10	Mind races thinking of many things at once
17. Feel empowered during change	0 1 2 3 4 5 6 7 8 9 10	Feel victimized during change
18. Recognize my strengths and capabilities when engaging in change	0 1 2 3 4 5 6 7 8 9 10	Engage in changes far beyond my personal capabilities
19. Spend time sorting out paradoxes	0 1 2 3 4 5 6 7 8 9 10	Spend time trying to keep things the same
20. Have happy relationships with friends	0 1 2 3 4 5 6 7 8 9 10	My friends and I stay in constant conflict
TOTAL		

SCORE	LIFESTYLE	CONDITION PATTERN
160-200	EXTREME ⟶	*Dis-ease*, anxiety, constant deadlines, worry, guilt, high stress, burnout, illness
130-159	FAR AWAY FROM HOME ⟶	Frequent deadlines, anger, frustration, vulnerability, fear, procrastination, insecurity, worry, avoidance of change
100- 129	AWAY FROM HOME ⟶	Imbalance, loneliness, inflexibility, denial, withdrawal
50-99	LEAVING HOME ⟶	Questioning, indecisive, dissatisfied, restless, distracted, searching for more
Less than 50	HOME ⟶	Balanced lifestyle, embracing change, enjoying inner peace, in harmony with self and others, little time pressure, relaxed, healthy, adaptable, happy, whole, feeling free

Where did you end up on the **Personal Lifestyle Assessment**™? *The Prodigal Principle* teaches us to stay aware of the signals that tell us it's time to change to a better way of life.

Keep in mind that you do not just wake up one morning with the flu. Do you remember the symptoms like runny nose and sore throat that alerted you before the advanced stage of flu?

Although a stroke hits suddenly, it doesn't come out of nowhere. Warning signs come — dimness or loss of vision, a sudden onset of blurred or double vision, memory loss. Also, numbness in the face, arms or legs, angina (chest pain), fluid retention and weight gain, excessively high blood pressure, or transient ischemic attack (TIA) or mini-stroke are clear quickenings that tell us it is time to change our lifestyles. When you choose to recognize these signals and begin constructive action, you can begin to heal. Choosing the right diet, exercising, eliminating negative stress, cultivating a positive mental attitude and controlling uses of drugs, alcohol and tobacco all help prevent strokes.

Something like bankruptcy is no different. Bills pile up. Creditors haunt you. Your income decreases. You face these warnings before bankruptcy court. When we have exhausted our lines of credit, charged our credit cards beyond the limit or are dodging collectors, we are receiving signals to seek guidance on budgeting and financial planning and learn the powerful principles of prosperity and plenty.

Take a heart attack. Your heart doesn't just jump up one day and attack you. You attack your own heart with bad habits including excessive intake of alcohol, high serum cholesterol, high fat content, high blood sugar levels and little exercise. Your heart gives you feedback — palpitations, chest pains, dizziness, leg cramps and excessive fatigue. Left unattended for too long, we wear down our immune system, stretch our heart beyond elasticity, erode our positive emotions and mask healing. In 1994, the American Heart Association reported that 1.5 million Americans would have heart attacks that year with two-thirds surviving. More than 3 million would live with angina (the intense chest pain caused by blocked coronary arteries). As for costs, angioplasty averages $20,000. Heart bypass surgery costs approximately $60,000. Ten to 12-week residential programs for heart recovery cost $5,000 to $7,000. Last year, Americans spent over $14 billion on heart surgery.

How many spouses are stunned when they find out that they are going to get a divorce? We are warned of separation or divorce — couples grow apart, they can't see eye to eye, they don't meet each other's expectations, the thrills and fun fizzle, they begin affairs.

Whatever the situation, these are signs telling us things have gone awry and that a particular area in our life is pushing us off balance. Lacking the awareness or the skills to set things right, we jeopardize our happiness and our well-being. Holding onto our extreme conditions is a luxury we can't afford.

✏ Use this *power practice*:

1. What is one of your current extreme conditions?

_____

_____

_____

_____

_____

2. What signals are telling you it's time to get out of this extreme condition?

_____

_____

_____

_____

_____

3. How do you plan to get yourself out?

_____

_____

_____

_____

_____

_____

_____

Chapter

7

A Frog in Time

*Why is it that fools always have
the instinct to hunt out the unpleasant secrets
of life, and the hardiness to mention them?*
— EMILY EDEN

W hen you have not had sufficient practice in listening
to warnings and taking timely, positive action, you will not know
how to change when a catastrophe strikes. Consider this simple
example from a junior high school biology experiment:

A frog jumps into a bucket of boiling water. He feels the heat
and jumps right out. Another frog sits in a bucket of cool water. A
fire is lit under it. The water turns from cold to cool to warm. The
frog continues to sit. The water gets hotter and begins to boil. Still
the frog sits. He has not adjusted to the changes surrounding him
and now that it is catastrophic, he can't hop out because he does not
have the energy and **he does not know *how* to get out.** (In 1984,
Noel Tichy and David O. Ulrich referred to this "boiled frogs"
phenomenon in their works on transformational leadership.)

The signals telling us we need to adjust to the changes around
us are called *quickenings*. These change triggers come to us as nudg-
ings, naggings, pains, good or bad news bulletins, intuitions, new

assignments, medical diagnoses, requests or as bits of constructive feedback from friends or family members. *Quickenings* may come as sudden whacks on the side of the head or may be absorbed gradually over time. *Quickenings* can be life-saving. They come to energize us and give us practice in managing the changes in our lives. They are essential to changing our awareness and our actions. When we ignore these signs or do not have the awareness to recognize them, we are doomed to their consequences. Once we are in the heat of catastrophe — whether related to our work, relationships with others or our health — we don't know how to get out.

In **Greg's** case, he failed to make timely, positive, personal and professional changes before his heart attack. He became so pacified by his couch potato state that he was not aware of the many nudges beckoning him out of his cocoon. He was *quickened* by catastrophe — a massive heart attack. Fortunately for Greg, he lived to change and successfully transform his lifestyle.

> *The voyage of discovery consists not in seeking new landscapes but in having new eyes.*
> — MARCEL PROUST

Chapter

8

The Prodigal Son

*A man (or woman) travels the world over in search
of what he (or she) needs and returns home to find it.*
— GEORGE MOORE

The story of the prodigal son helps us understand how we can face catastrophe and change and miraculously overcome them. The prodigal son grew up in a house bursting with prosperity, extravagance and wealth. There was nothing he could desire that was not already provided. By today's standards, this father would make the *Fortune* magazine's front cover of world billionaires. Seduced by appearances of a better life, the prodigal son gathered his inheritance and left home for greener pastures. He did not settle in a neighboring community, across town, in another state or on the opposite seashore. He traveled to a faraway place previously unknown to him. Over time he squandered his wealth, and one day found himself homeless, jobless and penniless. His desperation drove him to skid row, so much so that he was willing to eat pig slop and corn husks.

The prodigal son fell into an abyss of poverty, hunger, loneliness and self abasement. His awareness was stretched far beyond what he had once known. He found nothing in his outer world to heal him.

Shaken by his catastrophe, the prodigal son came to himself and decided to make a major life change. In his broken-down and unkempt condition, the prodigal son headed **home.** Had his friends seen him, they would not have recognized him. Although his physical appearance was wrecked beyond recognition, his father

recognized him from a far distance and welcomed him home lav-
ishly and unconditionally. Back in his father's home, the son was
restored, renewed, rejuvenated and refreshed. He was a changed
person — revived and ready to meet his new world.

Home is referred to frequently in this book. **Home** is used as
a metaphor to create a symbol for a state of mind. It is character-
ized by thoughts that keep us feeling confident, safe to live within
ourselves and assured to take charge of our own lives. At **home** we
live in a state of peace within ourselves, with others, and with life
and the life process. We love and approve of ourselves and we act
in loving ways toward others. At **home,** the state of mind creates
ideal conditions for:
- Peace   • Harmony   • Joy   • Love

Here are some *home tools*:

Your state of being at **home** gives you a treasure house teem-
ing with assurances of:
- Safety   • Security   • Abundance
- Trust   • Creativity

The human heart is the center of circulation. It carries what's in
your **home** to all parts of your body. **Home** and the human heart are
one. The condition of one's **home** affects the rhythm of the heart. As
your thoughts are in your treasure house, your home and heart work in
harmony to help you flow with streams of flexibility, ease, calmness, clarity, self-confidence and courage. As you meet circumstances, harmony
with **home** and heart helps you stay energetic, synergetic and well.

Many times we travel the world over to find home only to
return and find it within ourselves. Staying **home** keeps you aiming for worthwhile things versus constantly aiming for things that
only look like happiness. At **home** you find ways to face the positive side of change and keep growing. You can create for yourself a
safe and secure new future. You can use your mental state of **home**
to find contentment, create balance in your life and live peacefully
with yourself, your life and the life process.

Keep your home sound and whole; for as it is, so is your heart.

The prodigal son parable teaches us to use these *home tools*:

1. When we face what seem like the worst situations in life, we are still greater than our circumstances.
2. When we change our awareness to possibilities, we can change our circumstances.
3. Possibility thinking crafts solutions and turns dreams into realities. Old thought patterns and negative behaviors dissolve, creating room for new, healthier behavior patterns.

Here is some *power practice*:

1. Think about a time when you were in an extreme condition or felt at the end of your rope. Write about your memory of it.

_____
_____
_____
_____

2. What steps did you take to change the situation?

_____
_____
_____
_____

3. How did you resolve the situation?

_____
_____
_____
_____

4. What steps did you take to change your life?

_____
_____
_____
_____

5. Whom did you ask to help you?

_____
_____
_____
_____

✐ More *power practice*:

When you are aware of *quickenings,* clarify these questions so you can act on them:

1. What have I to lose?

_____
_____
_____

2. What have I to gain?

_____
_____
_____
_____

3. What is over?

_____
_____
_____
_____

4. What is not over?

_____
_____
_____
_____

5. How can I cherish and respect my past?

_____
_____
_____
_____

6. What pieces of the past can I keep and take with me through my transformation?

_____
_____
_____

Chapter 9

The Prodigal Journey

HOME
Phase 1
Phase 7

PHASE 1
HOME is a positive state of mind. At home, we are
balanced, peaceful and relaxed.

PHASE 2
LEAVING **HOME** is a restless state of mind. We are
questioning, dissatisfied, frustrated and indecisive.

PHASE 3
AWAY FROM **HOME** is a state of imbalance.
We refuse to return to positive, constructive thinking (**home**).

LEAVING
HOME
Phase 2

CLOSE
TO HOME
Phase 6

PHASE 4
FAR AWAY — LIVING IN THE EXTREME is a state of habitual negative
addiction. We practice fear, doubt, worry, guilt, anger. We seek peace through
food, alcohol, TV, drugs, work, others, sleep. We find our vulnerability.

PHASE 5
HOMESICK/HEADING **HOME** is a discontented state
of mind. We change our attitude and reclaim our goodness.

PHASE 6
CLOSE TO **HOME** is a renewed state of mind.
We believe in ourselves and build courage and confidence.

HOMESICK
HEADING HOME
Phase 5

PHASE 7
HOME AGAIN is a whole new lifestyle. Our positive
attitude is restored, reborn, rejuvenated.

AWAY
FROM HOME
Phase 3

FAR AWAY
(THE EXTREME)
Phase 4

Change your attitude and you change your destiny.

Understanding The Prodigal Journey

THE SEVEN PHASES OF AWARENESS

PHASE ONE

HOME
BALANCED LIFESTYLE
- Peaceful
- Harmonious
- Powerful
- Loved
- Whole
- Healthy
- Happy
- Free

PHASE TWO

LEAVING **HOME**
QUESTIONING BALANCE
- Dissatisfied
- Frustrated
- Restless
- Indecisive
- Distracted

PHASE THREE

AWAY FROM **HOME**
LOSING BALANCE
- Imbalanced
- Lonely
- Regressing
- Inflexible
- Denying
- Withdrawing

PHASE FOUR

FAR AWAY FROM **HOME**
OUT OF BALANCE
LIVING IN THE EXTREME
- Fearful
- Doubting
- Worrying
- Guilt-ridden
- Angry
- Withdrawing
- Self-abasing
- Anxious
- Frustrated
- Insecure
- Stressed-out
- Self-destructive

PHASE FIVE

A. **HOMESICK**
RECOGNIZING NEED
FOR BALANCE
- Quickening
- Longing for home
- Changing awareness
- Coming to oneself
- Looking for change
- Looking toward home
- Preparing for home
- Looking to future

B. HEADING **HOME**
- Creating new awareness (re-clarifying values)
- Expressing an ardent desire for change
- Setting clear direction
- Stating clear purpose
- Expecting the very best from self
- Acting on plans
- Practicing familiar successful lifestyle patterns
- Manifesting new lifestyle patterns

PHASE SIX

CLOSE TO **HOME**
REGAINING BALANCE
- "Home in sight"
- Seeing goodness
- Redefining self
- Accepting self
- Loving self
- Listening to self

PHASE SEVEN

HOME AGAIN
BALANCED
- Reborn
- Reinvented
- Refocused
- Rejuvenated
- Restored
- Manifesting new lifestyle patterns

By now you see the picture. The seven phases of the Prodigal Journey show us how we can change our view of our life and our world, turn our life around and get back in balance. We can use this model to find the positive side of change and live healthy, prosperous and successful lives.

✐ Here is some *power practice*:

Think about a time when you managed your way back **home** to peace, joy, harmony and a general state of well-being. Describe it. What phases were similar to the Prodigal Son's journey?

_____

_____

_____

_____

_____

_____

_____

_____

_____

_____

_____

_____

_____

_____

_____

_____

_____

_____

_____

_____

_____

_____

_____

_____

_____

_____

_____

_____

_____

_____

10

Reinventing Yourself

Even a thought, even a possibility can shatter us and transform us.
— FRIEDRICH WILHELM NIETZSCHE

A *transformation* creates a change in appearance, form, nature or circumstance. It is most dramatic in nature, changing the caterpillar to a magnificent butterfly; the egg to an eagle.

Transformation is triggered by *quickenings*. Transformations arouse, stir up, stimulate and motivate. They can change our vision, our values and our direction. Transformations spark creative energy, create new courage and craft unimaginable results. We go through many transformations in life, some lasting for a few days. Others such as healing a deep wound, changing a career or building a harmonious relationship can take one, two or even five years. It is most important that we lean into the transformation process and come through after completion. Only then do we bring out our true potential and find our strengths.

✐ Here is some *power practice*:

1. What are some transformations you have completed?

_____
_____
_____
_____

2. How did you feel after you had completed them?

_____
_____
_____
_____

The transformation cycle leads us to our new lifestyle.

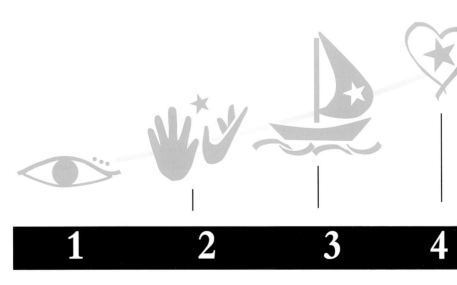*Home tools*:

Here are the eight steps of the transformation cycle:

1. **Create new awareness (re-clarify values).**
2. **Express an ardent desire for change.**
3. **Set clear direction.**
4. **State clear purpose.**
5. **Expect the best from yourself.**
6. **Act on your plans.**
7. **Practice familiar successful lifestyle patterns.**
8. **Manifest your new lifestyle.**

Just as the butterfly emerges by orderly sequence from its larval stage to its mature state, we too complete our transformations in an orderly step-by-step fashion. Ours begin with changed awareness. The eight steps of transformation — moving us from an extreme condition back **home** to balance — are reviewed in the next section.

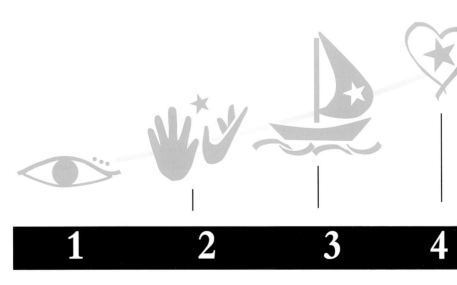

5   6   7   8

1. Create New Awareness

Like attracts like.

Your awareness governs your thoughts, conversations and actions. For example, when was the last time you bought a new car? Do you remember what happened once you decided what kind of car you were going to buy or when you drove the car off the dealer's lot? Automatically, you started seeing the same car, same make, same model, same color. Altered awareness sensitizes you to the sameness. Your awareness helps you turn your attention to information and data to be recalled, memorized, understood and applied. This is later translated to what you think, see, say and do. Sometimes, even in spite of empirical findings, the way we see information is based on our awareness.

Your awareness is you. How others see you is an outer reflection of your awareness — your inner world turned inside out. Everything we manifest and all of our results come through our awareness. If we want to see ourselves differently, we change our awareness. New awareness leads to new results.

When we create new awareness, we examine how we see ourselves in areas that carry themes of fear, crime, violence, security, loss of some kind, terror, pain, old age, poverty, loneliness and death.

Home tools:

• Change negative awareness to positive in these areas: personal achievement, love, beauty, equality, growth, power, self-esteem, contentment, life, peace, joy, happiness and self-satisfaction.

• Attempts to change our behavior by altering awareness have proven successful and sustaining. These approaches require discipline, practice and repetitive regimens of affirming the positive, telling ourselves we're okay, seeking the company of caring people and those who see us in a positive light. We must also monitor our friends and associates. Avoid or lessen contact with those who don't see the good in you.

We see as we believe; and we see the outer world as we see ourselves. Our outer world is a reflection of our awareness. In a Calvin and Hobbes cartoon, Calvin and Hobbes were watching television while commenting on all of the newspaper articles about violence on TV. Calvin talked about the few thousand homicides he had watched on TV, and he talked about his rights to watch violence on TV, express his views about TV and be catered to by the advertisers, because after all he was the customer. Hobbes asked him if he worried that all of the violence might be desensitizing, to which Calvin immediately retorted, "Naah, I'd like to shoot the idiots who think this stuff affects me." (Bill Watterson, August 29, 1994). Positive awareness is not abstract. It shows up in our actions. Keep your awareness positive to enhance your creativity, solve your toughest problems, know the desires of your heart and heal yourself.

✐ Here is some *power practice*:

1. List some ways you can use positive awareness in your life to prevent and overcome fear, depression, anger and anxiety. When we train ourselves to maintain positive awareness, we create ripe conditions for leading healthy, happy, whole, integrated and self-renewing lives.

We must be awareness vigilantes and constantly check our awareness and make timely adjustments. Ask yourself, "What is important to me right now? What awareness dominates my thoughts right now?" Get feedback from someone you trust and ask, "What do I seem to talk about most of the time? Do you hear any reruns? What do you see in my face (frowns, smiles, peace, wrinkles, anger) and posture (slumped shoulders, straight, erect back)?"

 *Home tools*:

Here are some additional tips to help you keep a vigilant awareness:

• Sharpen your intuition.
• Listen inwardly.
• Schedule quiet time and find a safe haven to spend time thinking. Ken is seldom without something to read in his hands. He wakes up in the morning and makes a beeline from the bedroom to the newspaper to the bathroom to sit and read. After bathroom duty, he goes to the kitchen table and continues reading while he eats breakfast. At lunch he reads novels. During the business day he reads financial reports. In the evening he watches TV for several hours and then reads murder mysteries before bedtime. The next morning the same routine begins all over again. Ken spends little time thinking, reflecting or listening to his own inner thoughts. Thinking time helps you know your own inner voice and trust yourself.
• Follow your instincts.
• Monitor what you think, see, say and do.
• Monitor your friendships and conversations with others.
• Stay aware of beauty and good in all creation.

> *You can observe a lot by watching.*
> — YOGI BERRA

2. Express Ardent Desire
When you find your will, you find your way.

You can use your changed awareness to create new desire. Begin your desire statements with "I want...," "I intend to..." or "I expect...." Relinquish all thinking that gets in the way of expressing your desire to manage yourself through change.

Some stuck-thinking statements are:

I'm not good enough.
I don't have enough money.
I come from the wrong side of the tracks.
I can't measure up.

Replace these stuck-thinking statements with ones that free you and help you visualize what you expect for yourself.

Home tools:

I am the best person to do this.
I am free and unlimited.
I am loved and supported by reliable loved ones and friends.
I am my very best friend.
I am strong.
I accept myself and acknowledge my talents.

Here is some *power practice*:

Write your own desire statements beginning with "I want" or "I intend to" or "I expect to." Review them over and over and believe in them as you see them. Feel them. Hear them. Get excited about them. Embrace them. Act on them.

_____
_____
_____
_____
_____
_____
_____
_____
_____
_____
_____

Your word is your wand.

3. Set Clear Direction

When you know which way you're going, you will find a way to get there.

Be specific as you determine which way you want to head in your new lifestyle. In the case of the prodigal son, he said, "I must go to my father's house." Pretty specific, wouldn't you say? Stating his desire clearly helped point him in the right direction and put him on a clear path back home.

Ann found herself unemployed for the first time in her 15-year career. To get reemployed, she had to write a winning resumé, market herself, interview effectively and project a positive image every day. After reading Ann's resumé, her employment counselor was completely confused. She asked Ann to tell her what kind of work she wanted to do. Ann answered, "I don't know." Her resumé reflected her indecision. Ann's counselor worked with her to describe her experiences, new work and skills portfolio. If you read her resumé now, you would know that she is the perfect contractor for a small business' software computer consulting needs.

Home tools:

- Rely on your own internal resources such as wisdom and creativity.
- Actively listen to the guidance that comes from within you.
- State your guidance.
- Write it.
- Rely on it.
- Set goals to set out in your new direction.
- Prioritize your steps.
- Write a time frame.

If you need help defining what you want or what direction to take, get help.

Some possible resources to consider are:

➠ Business development center such as U.S. Small Business Administration or Service Corps of Retired Executives Association (SCORE)
➠ Outplacement agencies
➠ A women's center on a college campus or at a YWCA
➠ On-line services such as America Online, AppleLink and CompuServe
➠ Associations such as National Association for the Self-Employed (NASE), National Association of Home-Based Business (NAHBB) or National Association of Women Business Owners (NAWBO)
➠ Join a business or professional group in your area of interest
➠ Join a Toastmasters or International Training in Communication organization for communication skills development
➠ Find a support group of like-minded people who can serve as catalysts, give feedback, support and leads in your area of endeavor
➠ Join a health club or physical fitness center
➠ Form a walking club or bicycling club

4. State Clear Purpose
When you know why, you will always find out how.

When you clearly state why it is important for you to change your behavior, you trigger a positive motivation for action. Clear purpose gives you a reason to change and follow your new direction. Knowing *why* stimulates action, excites you, creates passion and builds the energy you need to move forward.

Home tools:

As you state your purpose for change, know what is important for you in these areas:

- YOU (Put the oxygen mask to your face first.)
- Your loved ones and friends
- Your health
- Your finances
- Your work
- Your talents, skills and abilities

Here is some *power practice*:

1. Why is this change important to me (for my health, work, happiness, satisfaction and general well-being)?

_____
_____
_____
_____
_____

2. Why is it important to my family, loved ones or significant other(s)?

_____
_____
_____
_____
_____
_____
_____

3. What are some potential risks?

_____
_____
_____
_____
_____

4. What are the rewards?

_____
_____
_____
_____

5. What are some sensory images evoked by this change? What does it look like or feel like? How does it sound? Describe your movements toward the change. Draw pictures about this change and new direction.

_____
_____
_____
_____
_____

5. Expect the Best from Yourself
Believe in yourself and follow what makes you happy.
Your best is your belief that you hold the key to your greatness. When you believe the best of yourself, you know you can take the necessary steps to change your life.

Home tools:

Some of the *best* kinds of beliefs we can form about ourselves fall in these areas:

- High self-worth
- Love for others
- Harmony with self and the universe
- Love for self
- Wisdom to know answers
- Personal empowerment

*What is within you is far greater than
what you face outside of you.*

⬧ Here is some *power practice*:

1. Beginning with the words "I am," list your strengths.

_____

_____
_____
_____
_____

2. List the things you take pride in.

_____
_____
_____
_____
_____

3. Describe what excellence means to you.

_____
_____
_____
_____
_____

4. Describe what personal ethics means to you.

_____
_____
_____
_____
_____

5. Describe what showing love for others and living in harmony with the universe mean to you.

_____
_____
_____
_____
_____
_____

6. Act on Your Plans

Faith without great works is dead.

Vision, direction, purpose and plans go hand in hand. Your vision helps you see possibilities. It pulls you to your direction and helps you plan how to get there. Your direction helps you see the future. Your plans propel you and keep you pressing on toward your goals.

How many times have you ever heard people use these words?

• Woulda   • Mighta   • Coulda   • Shoulda

These words are used by people who had vision, desire, direction and purpose and were left sitting on the tarmac post afterburn. Desire must match direction, purpose and action. A true change agent acts on plans and gets things done.

⬬ *Home tools*:

Taking decisive and timely action helps you in these ways:

• Matches intentions with results
• Confirms the measurement standard so you can assess your results
• Helps you anticipate glitches, reactions and results and shake off SNAFU (situations normal all fouled up)
• Inspires you
• Builds confidence
• Uncovers new talents and abilities
• Opens doors to cooperation and partnerships with others
• Gives new meaning
• Builds commitment and loyalty to self

When you act on your plans, positive communication with yourself and others is essential. Here are some ⬬ *home tools* for you to use as you do some *home work* in the area of positive communication.

Negative communication creates stress and eventually conflict between two persons or a work team. Communicating negatively about yourself or your abilities and attributes also creates stress. Look at the word stress. Twist it and see it in a positive manner. Stress turned around with the letter *a* becomes *asserts*. When you assert yourself, you use positive communication for positive outcomes. You win, and so do others in the assertive communication process. The assertive communication model is the **AWARENESS PIE.** The letters in **PIE** stand for:

Perspective	**I**nspect	**E**xpect

Perspective involves understanding the situation and finding out how it affects you and others. As you gain perspective, listen inwardly, talk with others who love you and can give you honest feedback. Describe the situation in an objective manner. Now is not the time to write about how you feel. Just state the facts at this stage. Answer the question, "What is going on with me right now?" Describe the condition or situation.

When you **inspect**, you examine the situation as you have objectively described it. You investigate it, get more facts if necessary, study it and look at it carefully from several different angles. Inspect yourself as well. How can you see this situation in an objective manner?

Expect means you anticipate outcomes. Ask yourself what you want to come out of this resolution. Visualize it. Look forward to it. Confidently believe in it. Expect it. Know what you expect from yourself and others involved.

Here is your **AWARENESS PIE** illustrated.

You are at the center of your **AWARENESS PIE.** Once you have completed your **PIE** analysis, you are ready to commit to action. Your **PIE** analysis helped you take an inventory of yourself and the situation in a particular area of your life. Once you state the action you need to take, you are ready to write positive "I statements" to help inspire you to complete your plans. Write your "I statements" as though you have already accomplished them. This will set the energy and enthusiasm in motion with only the manifestation left to match your desire with your outcomes. Go around the **AWARENESS PIE** and write your descriptions in this order:

1. Describe your **sensations**. Twist your negative sensations and see, feel, hear and be in touch with yourself in a positive, productive manner. Write *I statements* such as "I am calm." "I am peaceful." "I am joyful." "I am confident." "I am healthy."
2. Describe what you **think** about your sensations. Begin with, "*I think* I am the best person to complete this plan."
3. Write about how you **feel.** Again, begin with *I statements.* State what you feel. "I feel excited." "I feel energetic." "I feel strong." "I feel enthusiastic." "I feel connected and self-assured."
4. Analyze what you **expect**. What do you intend to do about this situation? What do you expect as an outcome? Include a deadline.
5. List the **actions** you will take. Acting on your plans matches expectations with results. Write your action steps and follow through.

Review all areas of your life — family, financial matters, work, relationships and physical well-being, and begin to plan for peace by completing the awareness pie for positive communication and positive resolution.

Peggy's greatest need was in the area of physical well-being. She was overweight and suffered from high blood pressure. She met with a diet and nutrition counselor and developed a fail-proof plan of action to lose 30 pounds; however, the only exercise she got was picking up her plan and putting it down again with one excuse after another about why she didn't get started. After completing her objective **PIE** analysis, she decided that the only thing keeping her from executing her weight-loss plan was herself. She took time to recommit to action by describing her condition and her immediate actions. Here's what Peggy's **AWARENESS PIE** looked like:

1. I am a good person and deserve to look great and feel great. I see myself weighing 130, wearing a size 8 dress and having no more headaches. I like myself and treat myself well.
2. I think the new me is the best me. My plan is realistic, reachable, reasonable and resourceful. I am the best person to complete my plan.
3. I feel enthusiastic about the new me. I feel healthy, happy, whole, complete and free.
4. I expect to look in the mirror on Nov. 1 and smile as I approve of my size-8 figure. I expect to wear my size 8 dress to the charity ball on Dec. 11. I expect to hear many compliments from my friends at the ball. I expect to continue to maintain my 130-pound weight. I expect to quit taking high blood pressure medication by Sept. 1. I expect to continue following the steps to keep me weighing 130 pounds or less.
5. I act today. Today I begin my plan. I have a support team of people to inspire me, exercise with me, give me feedback, coach me, spur me on and celebrate each victory with me.

Peggy accomplished what she set out to do, and today she continues to follow her plan.

✐ Here is some *power practice*:

Complete the **AWARENESS PIE** for a condition or situation in a particular area in your life (family, work, business, relationship, intellectual arena, physical well-being).

Perspective

_____
_____
_____
_____

Inspect

_____
_____
_____

Expect

_____
_____
_____
_____

Write active "I statements" for your **AWARENESS PIE.**

I sense _____

I think _____

I feel _____

I expect _____

I act _____

7. Practice Familiar Lifestyle Patterns

The first great gift we can bestow on others is a good example.

— THOMAS MORRELL

While Kathy's two 6-feet-plus sons were home from school one summer, they asked her to go to the health club with them and shoot some hoops. Now, mind you, it had been over 10 years since she had had a basketball in her hands, much less played with one. To please them, she went anyway. At the beginning they sparred and joked around with each other about who was champ and chump. Soon, the familiar feel of the ball came back to Kathy. She was shooting two and three-pointers, dribbling and making foul shots in a single swoosh. The game came back to her and she was able to demonstrate amazing speed and coordination.

The same can be true for you. You have constructive built-in patterns that you never forget. They wait to serve you. Even after long dormant spells, they come back when you decide to take action. Some of these skills are riding a bicycle, driving a car, skating or swimming. Others are reservoirs of courage, strength, joy, love and wisdom. Even though you might be burned out, stressed out, out of balance in another extreme, you still have built-in patterns to help you get back in balance and in better control of your life. As you press through change, you restore those patterns and build new ones. Find them and use them. You can find them in all areas of your life — physical, mental, intellectual, emotional and social.

⬤ *Home tools*:

Here are some of the more general mental and emotional lifestyle patterns that we all have and can draw from as we make our way back to balance:

- Positive mental attitude
- Caring
- Persistence
- Reliability
- Inspiration
- Resilience
- Focus
- Mission

- Compassion
- Leadership ability
- Enthusiasm
- Belief in self
- Buoyancy
- Vision
- Purpose

Here are some successful lifestyle patterns you might want to consider for work:

➠ Take risks
➠ Recycle your talents, skills, experiences
➠ Turn hobbies into businesses
➠ Bounce back after failure
➠ Collect and frequently admire your symbols of success (trophies, blue ribbons, letters of appreciation, certificates, bragboast file, photos, thank yous, newspaper write-ups)
➠ Prosper by your mistakes
➠ Celebrate milestones and reward yourself

✐ Here is some *power practice*:

Write some of your own successful lifestyle patterns.

_____
_____
_____
_____
_____
_____

8. Manifest New Lifestyle Behavior

When you activate your ardent desire and accompany it with direction, purpose, specific plans and familiar lifestyle practices, you create great changes for yourself. The changes you make become visible through your actions and are known as manifestation — creating the visible from the invisible and matching expectations with end results. Manifestation helps us see the invisible — strength, courage, faith, power, wisdom and positive mental attitude. The visible demonstration could be a better job, a college degree, a new relationship, a new home, a new car, a healthy body or a new business. When visible reality matches your dreams, you manifest your true qualities. Manifestation completes the transformation process.

People who complete transformations say they always feel stronger, clear headed, more energetic and more creative than ever before. They experience miraculous enthusiasm and courage.

As harrowing as their transformations might have seemed, they say they would do it all over again because they learned many lessons about what they were made of:

- They faced fear and found courage.
- They faced feelings of inadequacy and found confidence.
- They faced stagnation and found creativity.
- They faced lack and found abundance.
- They faced loneliness and found friendships.
- They faced desperation and found hope.
- They faced failure and found prosperity.

They lived through their transformations and learned profound lessons: how to be true to themselves, what really matters in their lives and what their true life purposes are about. Champions of change also say they feel a desire to give in the same manner in which they have received. Their highest desire is to contribute to others and the world.

When you reach the manifestation stage of your change, you know it. Others know it, and most important, you show it. You serve as a role model to help inspire others as they manage change in their own lives.

Transformed persons learn to serve as volunteers and give enormous contributions to help enrich the lives of others. They become the backbones of communities. They adopt a selfless commitment to service and gain even greater perspective on what is important in their lives. They always feel they can do more and give more.

✐ Here is some *power practice*:

Describe what happened after your last transformation. Who was the new you? How did you feel? What did you do for yourself? What did you do for others?

_____
_____
_____
_____

It is essential for you to complete your transformation. When you finish, you will find yourself completely changed. You will find that a portion of you has died, but a new survivor has emerged with attributes and talents far superior to those previously known or used.

Go through your transformation. Build lifestyle success patterns. Be prepared to thrive in change. Emerge and show your greatness.

> *Inside my empty bottle I was constructing a lighthouse while all the others were making ships.*
> — C.S. LEWIS

Chapter

11

The Prodigal Daughter

Independence? That's middle class blasphemy.
We are all dependent on one another, every soul of us on earth.
— GEORGE BERNARD SHAW

The story you're about to read shows how **The Prodigal Principle** works in modern times to turn our lives around and help us adjust and take advantage of change. Until June 18, 1993, Hortense always took her life into her hands as one with a joy stick, playing a Nintendo game. She ran her department with the command of a modern-day Patton and wouldn't take "No" for an answer. Whether it was running her household or volunteer committees, she knew how to direct and get results. She set specific goals, pushed herself with dogged determination and achieved what she set out to do. In essence, she saw herself in control and found self-assurance with each milestone of success.

How quickly her charge waned when a brain-stem stroke eclipsed all self-managed control panels, command posts and activators. As the stroke disarmed her entire body, she recalls attempting a featherweight hand movement to beckon for help. Instead, what seemed like a 2-ton body lay prostrate, heavy and motionless, slipping into a fathomless pit of inertia.

The blur from unconsciousness to consciousness placed her awareness in a state of nothingness — no movement, no speech, no feeling, no physical pain. Her mind hurled with a frenzy of questions. She asked, "What happened? Am I going to live? How long will this last? What next? How have I been reduced from an acknowledged dynamo of success to a mere shell, living by sounds of silence and threats of oblivion? Why me?"

The stroke left Hortense paralyzed on both sides and unable to move anything — her lips, neck or vocal cords. Clothed in a diaper and a plain white cotton hospital gown, Hortense could no longer do anything for herself. She lay for hours and days on end with plenty of time to think.

As she released her grip on arrogance, false pride and a need for complete self-sufficiency, she learned that the things she emphasized most (independence, control, her opinions) became less important. Empathy, listening, loving and receiving love became more important. She recalls carrying a lot of excess baggage and said she learned the hard way how to unload. By then, she was ready to ask, "What now?"

She began in-hospital rehabilitation. Even some of the smallest tasks such as getting out of bed, dressing herself and brushing her hair felt monumental.

She learned how to reverse her unhealthy lifestyle patterns. Her determination and keen spirit were channeled in a positive direction to promote physical, mental, emotional and spiritual balance. Today, she practices staying healthy through consistent mental rehabilitation — keeping her thoughts positive and constructive. Her diet consists of the basics — high fiber, whole grains, vegetables, beans, brown rice and fresh fruit. Although she sometimes feels like a juggler, she keeps her diet, healthy mental attitude, exercise and values all in balanced perspective.

Hortense said that during her recovery, she practiced these habits and completed her transformation. She offers these to you:

→ Stay determined. Positive determination gets you to your healthy destination.
→ See life as a learning process.
→ Face all of your challenges.
→ Draw from a wellspring of all the good you know — supportive friends and family, intuition, humor, risk-taking, spiritual teachings and positive lifestyle patterns.
→ Forgive yourself and others — even though it might seem impossible to do.
→ Love yourself and others.
→ Show empathy and sympathy.
→ Unload excess baggage. Don't pick it up again.
→ Loosen up. Have fun. Release, relinquish, be resilient.
→ Follow Victor Borge's saying: *Laughter is the shortest distance between two people.*

As she completed her transformation, Hortense said it was like grabbing hold of the end of a rope and being pulled up a mountain, reaching the summit and finding goodness up there. When she looked down, she saw an abundance of good on the other side. It's been almost two years since her stroke. She continues to enjoy a healthy lifestyle, supportive friends and family and harmonious relationships.

Hortense said that what helps keep her going is a quote by Susan Thurman:

A person who belly-laughs doesn't bellyache.

Follow Hortense through each phase of her transformation.

THE PRODIGAL PRINCIPLE APPLIED

1. HOME	2. LEAVING HOME
Achieved business success	High-control person
Set goals	Wrong food
Established business plans	Little exercise
Organized work and activities	Overweight
(Aware of Good)	**(Making Unhealthy Choices)**

3. FAR AWAY FROM HOME (THE EXTREME)

Out of control
Negative patterns becoming magnified
Ignoring warning signs
Focusing on negative appearances
Suffering brain-stem stroke
(Practicing Unhealthy Habits)

4. HEADING HOME

Positive awareness	Loving
Releasing and letting go	Listening
Trusting	Learning
Forgiving	

(Practicing Healthy Lifestyle Patterns: New awareness; Expressing ardent desire; Setting clear direction and stating purpose; Expecting the best; Practicing familiar patterns; Acting on plans; Manifesting new lifestyle)

5. HOME AGAIN

Healthy lifestyle
Supportive friends and family
Harmonious relationships
Giving, receiving, sharing
Knowing
Rejoicing
Focusing on positives
(Reborn: Renewing, Rebuilding)

6. STAYING HOME

Healthy lifestyle
Rehabilitating thoughts and actions
Acting as role model for others
Harmonizing
Giving and receiving goodness
Listening
(Life-long learning)

Hortense sees herself as a brand new person — remade, refocused, renewed and even more prosperous than before. **Home** again, in a consciousness of new life and renewed thinking, she is encouraged, strong and peaceful. She knows that as she stays at **home,** she will continue to heal and prosper.

A point revisited:

It is essential for us to keep a vigilant eye on **home.** You will stay balanced in the throes of uncertainty. You will find solutions to your problems, stay focused on your goodness, sustain inner peace and build harmony with others. Our awareness is our world, and our awareness runs constantly. Keep a vigilant awareness of your thoughts, words and actions. Constantly ask yourself, "What am I aware of right now?," "Am I concentrating on goodness?," and, "What's important to me right now?" Take time to ask yourself these questions on a daily basis. Describe what you think and see; how you feel. See your movement toward making constructive changes. Write your own steps for change.

✐ Here is some *power practice*:

Chart yourself through one of your recent transformations. Include what was going on in your life at each phase (home, leaving home, away from home and so forth). Describe the steps of your transformation.

_____
_____
_____
_____
_____
_____
_____
_____

*And binding nature fast in fate,
let free the human will.*
— ALEXANDER POPE

Chapter

12

Staying Home

*Hold close your awareness. Guard it. Watch over it vigilantly, in the
morning, at noon and at night. Unguarded, it lies prey to wanton raiders
— slipping in like sleek eels, silent, smooth and swift. Hold every good
thought sacred. Keep your awareness positive. Give good thoughts perspective,
meaning and clarity. Give each a special place for your renewal,
enlightenment and change.*

Many find their biggest opportunity is in learning to
stay home. They say that had they practiced staying-home principles
in the first place, they would not end up burned-out, stressed-out,
out of balance and generally out of control. Many leave home
because the grass seems greener on the other side. On television
and in movies, we are bombarded with images that dazzle, glitter
and glow, and the promise of a better life lures us in and we can easily turn from within — away from our treasure houses.

Jill, a highly-paid executive in a pharmaceutical company, was
offered an even higher paying job in her company. This promotion
promised her countless material rewards — extended executive
club privileges, a bigger company car, trips around the world with
the international division, doubled shares of company stock, a cor-
ner office, shmoozing with many top corporate officers, luminaries
and statewide politicians — an executive's delight. She was ready
to jump at this juicy offer, but stopped to compare it with her personal goals. She knew she had decided to spend more time devel-
oping a healthy lifestyle for herself. She and her teenage daughter
were finally spending more time together. She wanted to take
some college business courses. She was learning to relax more.
The day before she was to accept the promotion, she declined. She
knew it would be more difficult to get out of it if she got herself

sucked in. Jill knew her essential goals and the importance she placed on her family, so she could decline with confidence. Jill said, "My strong sense of purpose and direction, clear vision, firm values and awareness of even higher ideals gave me the courage to stick with my plans. I felt free. Plus, I freed the position for another person."

Jill kept a vigilant awareness of good. She focused on her vision, her values, her purpose, her goals and her plans. Jill said, "One's unsteady awareness is what causes him or her to veer and look for something different in the first place." Jill further explained, "When one is faced with the greener grass, it is important to keep focused on the good you already have. Don't let greed, your ego, fame, self-aggrandizement, friends, big promises and other alluring appearances eclipse your vision and plans. Don't mask your judgment, emotions and senses with opinions from others. Take time each day and count things you are thankful for."

How many times have you allowed in unwelcome and unwanted visual, verbal and symbolic stimuli and given them rent-free dwellings in your conscious awareness? These invaders can easily influence our behavior when we are most vulnerable, in states of:

- Fear
- Stress
- Depression
- Despair
- Confusion
- Self-abasement
- Self-pity

- Denial
- Burnout
- Uncertainty
- Procrastination
- Withdrawal
- Bargaining with self
- Boiled frog syndrome

In transition — loss of job, loved one or status; major changes in relationships; substance abuse problems — we are particularly vulnerable; we are in recovery.

Camped in our subconscious, these strong beliefs and illusions act like family members, charismatic leaders, authority figures and cults, telling us what to do. Repeated orders cause us to follow them automatically. They tell us what to think, and we think it. They tell us to stop trying, and we shut down. Although they have more than worn out their welcome, we keep them around to make ourselves believe they are good for us.

💿 *Home tools*:

Here are **13 tried and true techniques** that work to help you practice **staying-home principles:**

1. **Keep a vigilant awareness** of signals and cues telling you you are leaving **home.** Constantly monitor what you are thinking, saying, hearing, seeing and doing.

2. **Stay aware of beauty, good and truth.** See beauty in art, nature and others.

3. **Keep vivid and visual plans** for what you are to accomplish. Keep constant reminders taped to your bathroom mirror, refrigerator or other places you see frequently. Review them daily.

4. **Avoid burnout.** Stay realistic. Keep your head in the clouds and your feet planted on the ground. Keep your goals at a stretch, but not out of reach. Get constant feedback from people you trust.

5. **Follow a daily exercise program.** You can walk, do stretches, jog, bike, swim.

6. **Eat healthful foods.** Cut out too much fat, refined flour, highly chemicalized additives, too much sugar, too much bad cholesterol. Eat more grains, beans and local fruit and green vegetables.

> *Tell me what you eat, and I shall tell you what you are.*
> — BRILLAT-SAVARIN

> *The best doctors in the world are Dr. Diet, Dr. Quiet, and Dr. Merryman.*
> — JONATHAN SWIFT

7. **Keep a healthy self-concept**, high self-esteem, and practice self acceptance. It's okay to tell yourself you are great. Now sincerely believe it.

> *So much is he worth as he esteems himself.*
> — FRANÇOIS RABELAIS

> *Nothing we ever imagined is beyond our powers,*
> *only beyond our present self-knowledge.*
> — THEODORE ROSZAK

The biggest belief you can have is a big belief in yourself.

8. **Keep your immune system strong and active** with huge doses of positive humor, plenty of regular exercise and proper nutrients. Throw a Happy Mirthday.

> *Frame your mind to mirth and merriment,*
> *which bars a thousand harms and lengthens life.*
> — WILLIAM SHAKESPEARE

9. **Keep high hopes, focused direction and clear vision.**

> *Without hope we live in desire.*
> — DANTE

10. **Keep a vigilant awareness on your "My" words**. (My ugly body, my arthritis, my cold, my flu, my bad job, my bad boss, my bad children, my bad company.) Make a habit of getting rid of negative words after the word "my." Use positive "my words" — my great work, my happy life, my healthy body, my beautiful face, my brilliant mind, my balanced life. Collect data and get feedback daily. Self-correct and self-adjust. You are a lifelong student in your growth in positive awareness.

11. **Cancel all marathon funerals** (continuing to bury the past only to turn around and dig it back up again and again). They keep you in debt to the past, keep you in constant conflict and stymie your progress.

12. **Connect with positive, like-minded people** who can encourage and support you as you make significant changes in your personal and professional life. **Connectedness** to others is central to our human experience. Humans are social creatures. We look to others for companionship, partnership and fellowship. In the business world we network to build contacts and alliances. Go beyond networking. Advance to a high level of *webbing*, establishing and nurturing personal and business relationships person-to-person, computer-to-computer, fax-to-fax, pager-to-pager and modem-to-modem through the global computer network. Tap in and *web* on the information superhighway.

   Connect with people all over the world. Get to know them. Learn where their needs and abilities match yours. Make them your world partners. Through *webbing,* you can put the world at your fingertips. Through Interactive TV and the information superhighway, Americans use invisible electronic webs to share information and exchange opportunities with others all over the world. They help each other solve problems and look for new solutions and otherwise get together while remaining far apart. The Telecommuting Advisory Council tells us today over 7 million telecommute world-wide; and twenty-five million will by the year 2000. Webbing connects us all in the circle of the world. Get online and web.

> *The first small sacrifice of this sort leads the way to others, and a single hand's turn given heartily to the world's great work helps one amazingly with one's own small tasks.*
> — LOUISA M. ALCOTT

13. **Change from an attitude of work** to an awareness of *worth*. An ability to see your *worth* helps you develop your strength and untapped talents. An awareness of your worth helps you see your need for service. Embrace lifelong learning, growing and self-renewal. When you put your heart,

mind, intellect and soul in even your smallest acts and deeds, you find your *worth* and you find your way. Your true wealth is in your *worth* and your service. As Bob Dylan said, "You've got to serve somebody." Therein you will find your true happiness and peace of mind. If you're not serving your own *worth*, who else is?

When we find our true worth our work will follow.

✐ Here is some *power practice*:

Write reminders you will use to stay **home**. Include ways you will use to keep up with trends, stay positive, stay prepared, stay energetic, stay flexible, be of service to others, encourage others, stay enthusiastic.

I don't know what your destiny will be, but one thing I do know: the only ones among you who will be really happy are those who have sought and found how to serve.

— ALBERT SCHWEITZER

Chapter

13

Securing Your Future

The purpose of life is a life of purpose.
— ROBERT BYRNE

The Prodigal Principle teaches us,
**When we reach an extreme condition in our life,
we are quickened to transform and heal.**

[Extreme Condition + Quickening = Transformation]

As you face the *de-jobbed* world of work, you can sharpen your tools to forge greater energy and enthusiasm. You can prime your creative resources and find ways to stay positive everyday. Stay aware of change and trends. Stay focused on your strengths. Believe in yourself. Remember, *As within, so without.* Build a lifetime portfolio for your *worth*, by putting your heart, mind and soul into what you do for yourself and others, and by staying connected. In your life, you will constantly face challenges and seeming impossibilities. Regard these as opportunities to build awareness. With practice, you will dig beneath the discord and find harmony, dig beneath the fear and find your true undaunted self.

By pressing into our transformations, we discover our greatness. We learn resilience and how to flow with the positive stream of life. We learn to successfully navigate the confluence of complexities, ambiguity and disruptions in our lives with a sincere belief in goodness. We achieve a balanced lifestyle when we maintain positive awareness, clear vision and clear purpose, expectations for the best in ourselves, ability to act on our plans, successful lifestyle patterns and the ability to match intent with action. As we emerge, darkness changes to light, ignorance to knowledge, disharmony to harmony, and *dis-ease* to general well-being and radiant life.

Transformation unites human will with the positive attributes in life. When this happens, we expand our creative capacity, accelerate our results and achieve beyond human imagination. Old habits die, and our new awakening promises new creation, new manifestation and a whole new life. Expect change. Face the positive side. Embrace it. Thrive in these trying times of constant change and you will excel, stay steps ahead and flourish.

✐ Master this *power practice*:

What steps will you take to ensure your employability and build a healthy lifestyle?

_____
_____
_____
_____
_____
_____
_____
_____
_____
_____
_____
_____

When you are willing to give up being a caterpillar, your life,
like the butterfly's, takes on a whole new form and a whole new meaning.

INDEX

ACKNOWLEDGMENTS

THE PRODIGAL PRINCIPLE:
The Essential Handbook for Personal
and Professional Change

Contributors:
The author gives special thanks to countless companies, executives and management persons who contributed to this handbook by sharing their enthusiasm, creative ideas, keen interest and technical assistance. Many of these individuals work in insurance companies, law firms and major corporations such as The Southland Corporation, American Airlines, Congress Rotisserie, Price Waterhouse, Advest, Phoenix Home Life, Coopers & Lybrand, CIGNA Healthcare, First National Bank of New England and Computer Services Corporation. Others are entrepreneurs, professionals and sales and marketing executives.

Editor:
Deborah Hornblow

Design and Typography:
Harry Rich Associates, Inc.

Technical Assistance:
Patricia J. Cousins
W. David Jones, Ph.D.
Brian Jud

THE PRODIGAL PRINCIPLE

User Registration Form

Use this *Prodigal Principle* User Registration Form to stay connected with new developments and resources of Worthshops™ International, Inc.

Mail to:
Education & Training Department
Worthshops™ International, Inc.
P. O. Box 7111
Bloomfield, CT 06002-7111
U.S.A.

Or Fax the form to:
203-243-2504

Or call
203-243-2524

KEEP TOP PORTION FOR YOUR RECORDS.

▲TEAR OFF AND MAIL TODAY. ▼

☐ I would like to stay informed of new developments and resources for managing personal and professional change. My special interest is

_____
_____
_____

☐ I would like to offer comments on *The Prodigal Principle Handbook*. (Mail your comments to Worthshops™ International.)

Name _____
Title _____
Organization_____ # of employees _____
Address _____
City _____
State/Prov _____ Zip Code_____
Phone # _____ Fax _____

The popular *Employee Workshop for Managing Personal Change* is built on the proven guidelines in *The Prodigal Principle*. Participants discover how to build on their best results. Use this form to also request information on *The Prodigal Principle 5-hour workshop*. Or call today for more details (203-243-2524).

THE PRODIGAL PRINCIPLE

☐ Please mail me additional copies of *The Prodigal Principle: The Essential Handbook for Managing Personal and Professional Change*. My check is enclosed (book price: $14.95).

☐ Please contact me about volume discount orders. Discover big savings. Your book price could be reduced.

To place orders, call 203-243-2524 or mail your order using this form. Orders may be faxed to 203-243-2504.

Name _____

Title _____

Organization _____ # of employees _____

Address _____

City _____

State/Prov _____ Zip Code _____

Phone # _____ Fax _____

P.O. # _____

ACT NOW!
Mail to:
Worthbooks™ Publishing Group, Inc.
18 Biltmore Park
Bloomfield, CT 06002-2141
U.S.A.

Applicable sales tax, shipping and handling charges will be added. Same day shipping available.

☐ MasterCard   ☐ VISA

Account # _____ Exp. Date _____

Name as it appears on card _____

Signature _____

TEAR OFF AND MAIL TODAY.